KIDS ON EARTH

Wildlife Adventures – Explore The World
Black Macaque - Indonesia

Sensei Paul David

COPYRIGHT PAGE

Kids On Earth: Wildlife Adventures - Explore The World

Black Macaque - Indonesia

by Sensei Paul David,

Copyright © 2023.

All rights reserved.

978-1-77848-203-8 KoE_WildLife_Amazon_PaperbackBook_Indonesia_black macaque

978-1-77848-202-1 KoE_WildLife_Amazon_eBook_Indonesia_black macaque

978-1-77848-431-5 KoE_Wildlife_Ingram_Paperbackbook_BlackMacaqueMonkey

This book is not authorized for free distribution copying.

www.senseipublishing.com

@senseipublishing
#senseipublishing

Synopsis

This book provides a unique look at the Black Macaque, a species of primate found only in certain parts of Indonesia. It explores 30 fun facts about these animals, from their diet and behavior to their habitat and conservation status. It also examines the history of the species, the threats they face, and the efforts to protect them. This book is perfect for children aged 6 to 12 who are interested in learning more about these fascinating animals.

Get Our FREE Books Now!

kidsonearth.life

kidsonearth.world

Click Below for Another Book In Each Series

senseipublishing.com/KoE_SERIES

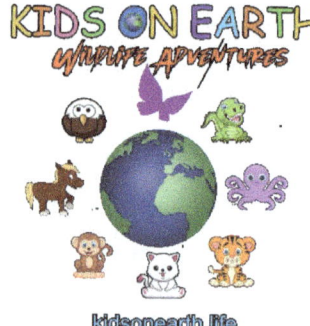

senseipublishing.com/KoE_Wildlife_SERIES

KoE En Español

senseipublishing.com/KoE_SERIES_SPANISH

www.senseipublishing.com

Join Our Publishing Journey!

If you would like to receive FUTURE FREE BOOKS and get to know us better, please click www.senseipublishing.com and join our newsletter by entering your email address in the pop-up box.

Follow Our Blog: senseipauldavid.ca

Follow/Like/Subscribe: Facebook, Instagram, YouTube: @senseipublishing

Scan the QR Code with your phone or tablet to follow us on social media:

Like / Subscribe / Follow

Introduction

Welcome to the fascinating world of the Black Macaque! These amazing animals are found only in certain parts of Indonesia, and they have some truly unique features that make them stand out from other primates. In this book, you'll explore 30 fun facts about Black Macaques, from their diet and behavior to their habitat and conservation status. You'll also learn about the history of their species, the threats they face, and what can be done to help protect them. So let's dive in and discover some amazing facts about these incredible animals!

The Black Macaque is also known as the Celebes Crested Macaque, or Macaca nigra.

They are the only macaque species native to Indonesia.

Black Macaques have a distinctive black crest of fur on their heads, and their fur is generally dark brown or black.

They are also threatened by habitat destruction, as forests are cleared to make way for agricultural land.

They have a diverse diet that includes fruit, leaves, insects, and even small vertebrates.

They are also known to use facial expressions to convey emotions.

13

They have been known to use tools, such as rocks and sticks, to open food items or to defend themselves.

Black Macaques are polygamous and males compete for mates.

They inhabit a variety of habitats, including tropical rainforests, mangroves, and secondary forests.

They are active during the day and sleep in the trees at night.

Black Macaques have a lifespan of up to 25 years in the wild.

They are listed as Vulnerable on the IUCN Red List of Threatened Species.

25

The biggest threats to Black Macaque populations are deforestation, hunting, and the illegal pet trade.

In certain areas, they are also hunted for their meat, which is considered a delicacy.

They are omnivores and have been known to raid crops of local farmers.

Black Macaques are protected by law in Indonesia, but illegal hunting still takes place.

There are currently around 2,500 individuals left in the wild, making them Critically Endangered.

Black Macaques are highly intelligent animals and can be trained in captivity.

Black Macaques are excellent climbers and can often be seen moving through the trees.

Male Black Macaques are larger than females, and can reach a weight of up to 30 pounds.

They are the most terrestrial of all macaque species and spend much of their time on the ground.

In captivity, they eat a variety of fruits, vegetables, nuts, and insects.

Black Macaques are very vocal animals and use a variety of calls and gestures to communicate.

They are highly social animals and live in troops of up to 30 individuals.

They usually give birth to one baby every two years.

Young Black Macaques stay with their mothers until they are around two years old.

53

Black Macaques are found mainly in the northern and eastern parts of Sulawesi, Indonesia.

They are also found in small parts of the neighboring islands of Buton and Muna.

There are currently several conservation efforts in place to protect Black Macaque populations.

The Black Macaque is an important species to the people of Indonesia, and its protection is essential for the health of the local environment.

Conclusion

The Black Macaque is an incredible species that is only found in certain parts of Indonesia. From their unique appearance to their social behavior and intelligence, these animals have many fascinating features. In this book, you have explored 30 fun facts about Black Macaques, from their diet and habitat to their conservation status and the threats they face. We hope you have enjoyed learning about these amazing animals and that you now have a greater understanding of the importance of protecting them for future generations.

Thank you for reading this book!

If you found this book helpful, I would be grateful if you would **post an honest review on Amazon** so this book can reach other supportive readers like you!

All you need to do is digitally flip to the back and leave your review. Or visit amazon.com/author/senseipauldavid click the correct book cover and click on the blue link next to the yellow stars that say, "customer reviews."

As always...

It's a great day to be alive!

Share Our FREE eBooks Now!

kidsonearth.life

kidsonearth.world

Click Below for Another Book In Each Series

senseipublishing.com/KoE_SERIES

senseipublishing.com/KoE_Wildlife_SERIES

KoE En Español

senseipublishing.com/KoE_SERIES_SPANISH

www.senseipublishing.com

www.senseipublishing.com

@senseipublishing
#senseipublishing

Check out our **recommendations** for other books for adults & kids plus other great resources by visiting
www.senseipublishing.com/resources/

Join Our Publishing Journey!

If you would like to receive FREE BOOKS and special offers, please visit www.senseipublishing.com and join our newsletter by entering your email address in the pop-up box

Follow Our Engaging Blog NOW!
senseipauldavid.ca

Get Our FREE Books Today!

Click & Share the Links Below

FREE Kids Books

lifeofbailey.senseipublishing.com
kidsonearth.senseipublishing.com

FREE Self-Development Book

senseiselfdevelopment.senseipublishing.com

FREE BONUS!!!
Experience Over 25 FREE Engaging Guided Meditations!

Prized Skills & Practices for Adults & Kids. Help Restore Deep Sleep, Lower Stress, Improve Posture, Navigate Uncertainty & More.

Download the Free Insight Timer App and click the link below:
http://insig.ht/sensei_paul

About Sensei Publishing

Sensei Publishing commits itself to help people of all ages transform into better versions of themselves by providing high-quality and research-based self-development books with an emphasis on mental health and guided meditations. Sensei Publishing offers well-written e-books, audiobooks, paperbacks, and online courses that simplify complicated but practical topics in line with its mission to inspire people toward positive transformation.

It's a great day to be alive!

About the Author

I create simple & transformative eBooks & Guided Meditations for Adults & Children proven to help navigate uncertainty, solve niche problems & bring families closer together.

I'm a former finance project manager, private pilot, jiu-jitsu instructor, musician & former University of Toronto Fitness Trainer. I prefer a science-based approach to focus on these & other areas in my life to stay humble & hungry to evolve. I hope you enjoy my work and I'd love to hear your feedback.

- It's a great day to be alive!
Sensei Paul David

Scan & Follow/Like/Subscribe: Facebook, Instagram, YouTube: @senseipublishing

Scan using your phone/iPad camera for Social Media
Visit us at www.senseipublishing.com and sign up for our newsletter to learn more about our exciting books and to experience our FREE Guided Meditations for Kids & Adults.

www.ingramcontent.com/pod-product-compliance
Lightning Source LLC
Chambersburg PA
CBHW080615110526
44587CB00040BB/3726